WELCOME TO WACKY HISTORY STORIES FOR KIDS

Lunar Press is a privately run publishing company which cares greatly about the accuracy of its content.

If you do notice any inaccuracies, or would like to discuss anything else about the book, then please email us at lunarpresspublishers@gmail.com.

Enjoy!

© Copyright 2023 - All rights reserved.
The content contained within this book may not be reproduced, duplicated or transmitted without direct written permission from the author or the publisher.

Under no circumstances will any blame or legal responsibility be held against the publisher, or author, for any damages, reparation, or monetary loss due to the information contained within this book, either directly or indirectly.

Legal Notice:
This book is copyright protected. It is only for personal use. You cannot amend, distribute, sell, use, quote or paraphrase any part, or the content within this book, without the consent of the author or publisher.

Disclaimer Notice:
Please note the information contained within this document is for educational and entertainment purposes only. All effort has been executed to present accurate, up to date, reliable, complete information. No warranties of any kind are declared or implied. Readers acknowledge that the author is not engaged in the rendering of legal, financial, medical or professional advice. The content within this book has been derived from various sources. Please consult a licensed professional before attempting any techniques outlined in this book.

By reading this document, the reader agrees that under no circumstances is the author responsible for any losses, direct or indirect, that are incurred as a result of the use of the information contained within this document, including, but not limited to, errors, omissions, or inaccuracies.

Contents

Who Was Wrestling Champ in 1830?	6
Who Discovered America?	10
Who Was the World's Most Successful Pirate?	14
Who Knows Where an Eel Hides Its Privates?	18
Who Ran the First Marathon?	22
Who Fought the Shortest War in History?	26
Who Could Have Stopped the Black Death?	30
Who is the Richest Person in History?	34
Who Introduced Hippos to Colombia?	39
Who Was the Only Person Both a Dwarf and a Giant?	41
Who Was the Real Cleopatra?	46
Who Were the Other Species of Human?	49
Who Were the Rock Stars of the Roman Empire?	54
When did Animals Have Jobs?	57
Who Stole Albert Einstein's Brain?	61
Who Could Predict the Future?	65
What is the Grossest Story in History?	70
Conclusion	72
Glossary	73

Introduction

History can often be a cruel and nasty thing to learn about, with wars and death staining it all the way back to the first time someone wrote it down on a tablet (not an iPad!). But even though this may be true, there were also so many wonderful things that happened too. But we're not here to stress over learning, and even though you will pick up some brilliant and useful knowledge along the way, we also want to have a little fun.

How can learning be fun, I hear you ask? Well, for me, learning is always fun. Knowledge is the most rewarding thing in the world, and it helps us to grow as a person. History is vitally important. If we don't know where we came from, then how will we ever understand where we want to be in life?

Anyway, when we are about to learn about the true richest person in history, Abraham Lincoln being a wrestling champ, and a man who ate dinner with his horse, then we are clearly in for a fun time!

Learning new things is always great, and when it is done in an enjoyable environment, then all the better, right? Sure, some subjects in school won't always be your favourite, but the ones that are should be a pleasure and something you look forward to each day.

This book is aimed at the latter, and if you picked it up in your local bookshop or got it on Amazon, it is because you are interested in learning about some weird and wacky parts of history. If you got it as a gift and this isn't what you would call interesting, then I'm sorry your auntie did that to you. She was only trying to be nice!

So, who here knows who fought the shortest war in history or who introduced hippos to Columbia? Who ran the first marathon (and dropped dead seconds later!), and who was the real Cleopatra?

If you know the answers to these questions already, then fair play to you. If you don't, then let's delve into this book together and learn some wonderfully weird and wacky historical facts!

Who Was Wrestling Champ in 1830?

This one is a real surprise, as when we think of wrestlers, we instantly imagine the shining lights and packed stadiums of the WWE. We picture legends of the ring such as Roman Reigns, Hulk Hogan, The Rock, and Stone Cold Steve Austin. But back in 1830, when wrestling was all grappling and rolling around in the mud, the county champion of New Salem, Illinois, was a 21-year-old man named Abraham Lincoln.

Of course, he would go on to become the 16th president of the United States, and probably the most famous one too. But before he was involved in politics, Honest Abe was a much feared and highly skilled wrestler.

Born into poverty in Kentucky in 1809, Abraham Lincoln's family struggled even to put food on the table. This would mean that he would have to educate himself, with his family far too poor to afford to send him to school. All through his life, Abraham Lincoln was an **avid** reader who loved nothing more than learning something new each day.

By the time he was 19, he had grown to be six foot four. Through his years of working the fields, young Abe had developed a strong, wiry, and muscular frame. Over the next few years, he was known to have had many wrestling matches, keeping a perfect record throughout them all. Famous for his honesty during his bouts, Abe was loved for his fairness, often stopping the fight when his opponent was too hurt to continue.

At the age of 21, Abraham was working in a local store in New Salem. The man who owned the store soon began promoting his star employee as the greatest wrestler in town.

Now, this was before microphones, so the news had to be spread verbally. It worked, and soon there were hundreds of people turning up each week to watch the young superstar, Abraham Lincoln, wrestle his way to fame. But one man didn't like what he was hearing, and soon Jack Armstrong—the champion and much-feared wrestler—wanted a piece of the young hotshot everyone was talking about.

He challenged Abe to a fight, and the bout was arranged. Not long into it, 21-year-old Abe was getting the better of his older opponent. This came as a surprise to some. As the crowd began to cheer Abe's name, Jack Armstrong became more and more desperate, and he was soon using illegal tactics, such as low blows and eye-gouging.

Abe could have gotten angry at this and decided to cheat too, but as he would always do throughout his life, he played fair and honestly. Using all of his strength, the future president lifted the massive Jack Armstrong over his head and slammed him onto the dirt, knocking him out. Honest Abe was named county champ in front of the adoring crowd—an honour he would carry proudly.

Two years later, when Abe was serving as a captain in the Illinois Volunteers, he was challenged by a man from another regiment. Never one to back down from a fight, he agreed to a match and would record his one and only loss in more than 300 contests. Ever the gentleman and understanding that he had lost to a stronger and more skilful opponent, Abraham Lincoln began calling himself the second-best wrestler in the state.

As his wrestling career ended, Abraham Lincoln swapped the ring for the bar. He opened up a saloon with his good friend W.F. Berry. They called it simply "Berry and Lincoln." Honest Abe was as shrewd a businessman as he was a lawyer, wrestler, and president, but his partner wasn't. Soon Mr Berry had spent any profits they might have made, and the business was ruined.

Never one to quit, Abraham Lincoln turned his attention to politics, and the rest, as they say, is history. There would be some bumps along the road, but everything else the 16th president accomplished was amazing. He would free the enslaved people, sign an Act that allowed poorer people to make a living, set up numerous universities, and establish the US banking system we know today. He also oversaw the end of the American Civil War.

Six days after the end of the Civil War, Abraham Lincoln was **assassinated** by John Wilkes Booth as he attended a play at the Ford's Theatre, in Washington, DC. News of his death spread through America and the rest of the world. Everyone mourned the passing of the man who is widely considered to be the greatest president the United States has ever seen.

But we are here to remember all of the good in his life and, of course, the astonishing wrestling career of Honest Abe. So, the next time you tune in to WWE to watch your favourite wrestlers in action, remember that before John Cena and Rey Mysterio, there was a 21-year-old champion who defeated all who came before him. His name was Abraham Lincoln: wrestler, bartender, war hero, president.

Did you know?

Abe wasn't the only president with a former job worth mentioning. Did you know that Ronald Reagan used to be a lifeguard? In his home-city of Dixon, Illinois, a young Ronald spent seven summers as a lifeguard - he rescued 77 people in total!

U.S President Lyndon B. Johnson had some experience in leading a large population, as his first job was as a goat herder on his uncle's farm in Texas. I wonder which one was easier.

President of Ukraine, Volodymyr Zelenskyy, once starred in a popular Ukrainian television series called 'Servant of the People'. His character was ... the President of Ukraine! Maybe he had such a good time pretending he decided to make it a reality.

British Prime Minister Tony Blair was once a stand-up comedian and lead singer of a band called 'Ugly Rumours' during his time at Oxford University. Apparently he didn't quite have the knack for performing...

This one is probably the strangest of them all. Pope Francis, head of the Catholic Church, used to be a nightclub bouncer. As in the big, scary man who prevents troublemakers from entering the building. He had quite the career change, but as a young student in Buenos Aires, he did what he could to make ends meet.

Who Discovered America?

For most people, the answer to this question seems simple, but in truth, it is far different. In school, kids across the globe are taught that the answer is, of course, Christopher Columbus. But did you know that nearly 500 years before Columbus was even born, a Viking explorer named Leif Eriksson navigated the tricky Atlantic waves to drop his anchor off the coast of North America?

But before we get into that, we must understand that his 'discovery' is not as clear cut as all that. For one, there were already people living in America—Native Americans—and they are thought to have walked there from Asia almost 13,000 to 35,000 years ago!

You may ask how this is possible when there is a sea between Asia and America. Well, it is said to have occurred during the Ice Age, when there would have been a landbridge formed in ice across the Bering Strait, the small body of water between Siberia and what is now modern-day Canada.

So, when we debate who the first person to discover America was, it is probably better if we think of it as who discovered it after the Native Americans had made it their home! Either way, the idea of someone crossing the Atlantic in boats made in 1000 AD (in the case of Leif Eriksson), or even the late 1400s (Columbus), is staggering, to say the least. We can only imagine the great mixture of wonder and fear they and their crew must have felt as they prepared to set sail into the unknown.

Leif Eriksson was born in 970 AD to Thjodhild and Erik Thorvaldsson, better known as Erik the Red. His father, who had been raised in Iceland, found himself banished to the unknown and icy Greenland around the time of Leif's birth. As the story goes, on Erik the Red's later return to the more **habitable** Iceland, he told the natives there—fellow settled Vikings from Norway—that the land he had founded was wondrous and full of vast fields and plant life. He called it 'Greenland' to tempt them even more (knowing it was mostly covered with ice, the sneaky git!). He hoped that more people would join him in settling there.

Around this time, in the year 986 AD, a Viking explorer named Bjarni Herjólfsson was sailing with his crew on a routine voyage from Iceland to Greenland. On their way, the boat was blown off course, and faced with strange waters, Bjarni ordered his crew to sail onward regardless.

When they saw a coastline they didn't recognise, he made a note of the coordinates without ever docking, turned around, and tried for Greenland again.

This time they were successful. When they docked, Bjarni spoke to Leif and many others of the strange land he had spotted in the west. Intrigued, the adventurous Leif Eriksson purchased Bjarni's ship from him. He gathered a crew of around 35 and set sail in search of the wondrous land his fellow Viking had seen. His father, Erik the Red, had been due to travel with him, but after falling off his horse on the day of the departure, he decided against it as he saw it as a bad omen. The Vikings, like many **dynasties** throughout history, were **superstitious.**

With Bjarni's hand-drawn map, Leif Eriksson travelled across the Atlantic Ocean. The first land he found was a barren and rocky place he named Helluland—which means Land of Flat Rocks in **Nordic.** This is thought to be modern-day Baffin Island. Here, Leif might have been tempted to turn around, believing Bjarni's sighting to be nothing more than a pile of rocks.

Instead, his adventurous spirit drove him to push on, and after discovering more islands, he finally anchored his boat and set foot on North American soil for the first time. It is believed now that this place was modern-day Cape Porcupine, Labrador, on the southeast coast of Newfoundland. After sending his crew on expeditions deeper into the new land they had discovered, they found it to be rich in grapes, with vines growing all around.

With this in mind, Leif Eriksson named it Vinland, which translates as 'Wineland.' Leif and his crew would spend the winter there, fishing for salmon, which were plentiful, and building their first settlement.

When the winter had passed, Leif returned to Greenland in the spring, bringing piles of grapes and timber from his findings. He would amazingly come upon an Icelandic castaway and his crew during this voyage and save them. This earned him the nickname Leif the Lucky.

Once back in Greenland, Leif met a noblewoman named Thorgunna and fell in love. They had two sons together—Thorgils and Thorkell—and he never returned to Vinland, the country we now know as Canada.

Other Greenlanders did, though. In the early 1960s, Norwegian explorer Helge Ingstad and his wife, archaeologist Anne Stine, uncovered a Viking settlement on the northern tip of Newfoundland. They proved once and for all that the **Norsemen** did officially discover America over 500 years before Christopher Columbus!

Did you know?

Not only were the Vikings the first to discover America, they are also thought to be the first to invent skiing. I'm sure it was great fun, but it was also a convenient way to get around in their snowy landscape. They even had a god of skiing - Ullr.

35% of the male population in Norway, Denmark and Sweden descend from Vikings. 1 in 33 men in Britain have Viking ancestry.

Six of our days of the week are named after Viking gods! They were influenced by the Romans, who named the days after the sun, moon and five planets (who were also gods). When they transferred these names from Roman into Norse gods, the days of the week we use today were created. It started with the Sun (Sunday), followed by the Moon (Monday). Then Mars, the Roman god of war, became Tyr, the Norse god of war (Tuesday). The Roman god Mercury became Odin, the wisest of the Norse gods (Wednesday). Then, Jupiter, the Roman god of lightning, became Thor (Thursday). Lastly, Venus, the Roman god of love, became Frigg, the Norse goddess of marriage (Friday).

Who Was the World's Most Successful Pirate?

Was it Blackbeard? Maybe it was Captain Kidd, the Scottish pirate who captured one of the Queen's ships in 1698? Or was it Sir Francis Drake, the nobleman who chose piracy over luxury upon the land?

These are all the names we automatically associate with pirates and the high seas, but the most successful pirate—by a long, long way—was not even a man. She was not even European, where most of the pirates in history usually came from. No, the most important and clever pirate to ever sail the seas and strike terror into all they encountered was a Chinese woman named Zheng Yi Sao (also known as Madame Zheng).

Zheng Yi Sao was born in the coastal province of Guangdong in 1775. Guangdong was and still is a bustling area of land on the northern tip of China. These days, the population is a staggering 126 million. Back in the 18th century, it was one of the busiest ports in the world, which made it a perfect place for pirates to steal and plunder!

Zheng Yi Sao was born into **poverty,** and she spent most of her early adulthood working in the back streets and in the floating gambling huts on the coast. When she met her future husband, Zheng Yi, he introduced her to the adventurous and dangerous life of piracy. They fell in love and were soon married. This was in 1801, and Zheng Yi Sao instantly joined her husband on his ship (this is also when she took his name).

Around that time, local rebels in Vietnam (China's neighbour) had taken charge. These locals were soon at war with the much more powerful China.

Now, did you know that most pirates didn't work as independently as some people might think? They were usually hired by noblemen and politicians to do their dirty work. The pirates were usually paid with a percentage of whatever they stole. This could be gold, spices, money and anything else they had been hired to take.

Well, Madame Zheng's husband was no different, and even though he was Chinese by birth, when the Vietnamese offered him money and ships to raid the Guangdong coast, he agreed to the deal. Like most pirates, Zheng Yi and his new wife believed that they didn't belong to any one country.

Although the raids were initially successful, at least for the pirate fleet, China was too strong for Vietnam. When the Chinese invaded them not long after, Vietnam had no choice but to surrender. This left Zheng Yi Sao, her husband, and their fleet of pirates **ostracised** from both countries, making them officially pirates in the way we understand them to be today.

Now, usually, when a fleet of pirates have completed whatever job they have been paid to do by governments or wealthy businessmen, they **disband**. But the Zhengs saw things differently, and they called a meeting among the many men and women who had sailed alongside them. Soon they had agreed that joining forces was their best option. By the time they were ready to sail again, they had 800 large boats, 1,000 smaller vessels, and 70,000 pirates at their disposal. These were split into six fleets, all with different coloured flags flown to represent them. The two most influential fleets were the Red Flags and the Black Flags.

Over the next few years, the pirate fleets were led by Zheng Yi Sao's husband, but in 1807, he fell overboard during a storm and died at sea. Without hesitating, Zheng Yi Sao took control of the fleet. There may have been some grumblings among the men, but Madame Zheng acted quickly. She took the young captain, Zhang Bao, of the mighty Red Flag Fleet as her new husband.

Again, the Flags were united, and they continued to pillage ships and coastlines, work for hire, and dominate the oceans for many, many miles all around. This raised concerns among the Chinese government, as Madame Zheng's fleet of pirates was practically becoming a state of their own. Madame Zheng even drew up a Code of Laws among her people, which among other things, was very insistent on women's rights. This, of course, was long before women's rights were rarely ever considered, proving once again that Madame Zheng was not only a pirate feared by everyone but a revolutionary thinker too.

But this is also the part in the story where Madame Zheng, also known as Zheng Yi Sao or Shi Yang, separates herself from most pirates throughout history. She did this with one simple decision: She knew when to quit. Unlike most pirates we know of who end up being hanged or sent to prison, Madame Zheng cut a deal with the Chinese authorities before everything fell apart.

The Chinese were more than happy to agree to peace, as up until that point, even the mention of her name was enough to strike fear into the bravest of soldiers.

In this deal, she and her new husband were allowed to live on land and, more importantly, in peace. This is called 'amnesty,' and in her written contract, Madame Zheng agreed to dismantle most of her fleets.

Again, this sort of peaceful end to piracy is basically unheard of, but it only went to show the intelligence and cunning of Zheng Yi Sao.

Her second husband, Zhang Bao, died while serving in the Chinese navy in 1822—ironically fighting pirates on behalf of the government. Madame Zheng moved back to Guangdong with her 11-year-old son and set up a successful gambling house. She lived out the rest of her days in peace and died at the age of 69. Much like everything she did in life, Zheng Yi Sao finished her time on Earth on her own terms.

Did you know?

Pirates did in fact wear eye patches, but not because they were missing an eye. To help their eyes adjust quickly between the darkness below deck and the brightness above, they covered one eye so it was always adjusted to darkness.

And there you have it. The greatest pirate in history wasn't Blackbeard or even Johnny Depp! It was a Chinese woman named Zheng Yi Sao who, at the height of her powers, made whole nations tremble at the knees. No pirate had ever come close to matching the sheer size of her fleets, and when the Red, Black, Blue, Yellow, Purple and White Flag Fleets were seen on the horizon, the terrified people on the shore knew they were staring at piracy greatness!

Who Knows Where an Eel Hides Its Privates?

You knew this look at history we are embarking on would be weird and wacky, right? Well, here is a question that has boggled the minds of some of history's brightest men and women for centuries: If eels can reproduce, then where does an eel hide its privates? And to make it even more mysterious - what does this have to do with the Bermuda Triangle?

We all know that for animals to have babies, there normally has to be a male and a female of the species, right? And usually, one will have male reproductive organs, and the other will have female reproductive organs, yes? Still, up until recent times, **zoologists,** scientists, and even the world's most famous **psychiatrist** struggled to understand how the common eel could reproduce when nobody could find the male eels' testicles!

Now, many of you may giggle at the mention of this body part that half the humans and creatures on this Earth have. But we all know they are there and what they do, so let's push on with this admittedly bizarre yet funny lesson!

You may be wondering why we are mentioning a psychiatrist when we are discussing eels and their you-know-whats, but before he dedicated his life to exploring the human mind, Sigmund Freud was also a student of zoology, among other things. He was a very smart man who devoted his life to studying how the mind works and trying to help those who suffered from depression to find their happiness.

Born in Moravia, a small town in the modern-day Czech Republic (it was then in the Austrian Empire), Sigmund was the youngest of eight children. He showed signs of his genius early on in his life, and at the age of 17, he was accepted into the illustrious University of Vienna. There, he would study many different subjects, including, of course, psychology.

But at the age of 19, young Sigmund wanted only to study eels and, more importantly, how they could have babies when the male had no testicles (no giggling!). He would spend his mornings on the beaches of Trieste, waiting to meet the fishermen as they came to shore with their catch. Then he would buy eels from them by the dozen.

Once Freud had his eels, he brought them home to the small laboratory he had set up in his home. Then he spent the rest of the day dissecting one after the other in search of those two little testicles that would put his mind at ease. Only scientific evidence would ever put his mind at ease, and the more he sliced open the eels and discovered no testicles, the more he became obsessed with finding them.

Many great men and women before and after Sigmund Freud had studied the habits when trying to answer the same question, and none had ever come up with any solid answers. No sightings of the eels mating had ever been confirmed. Even more bizarrely, no answer could be given as to how they could survive for long periods of time in areas that had no water close by.

While the doctors across the world pondered over this enigma, the eels were making their way to the centre of the Bermuda Triangle; an area in the Atlantic Ocean where many ships and planes had mysteriously disappeared...

Sigmund Freud never did discover how eels could reproduce without private parts, but thanks to modern science and technology, the question has finally been answered!

Up until recently, people had believed that several types of eels were different species. In fact, they were one and the same creature. The common eel is actually what scientists call an animal of **metamorphosis.** This basically means it can transform itself into something that looks and acts totally different to its original form (think of a caterpillar turning into a butterfly). Over the course of their long lives, eels will change into four different types of animals!

They start off as a larva with googly eyes, drifting on the open sea toward Europe. Then they morph into an almost transparent eel of only a couple of inches in length, shimmering their way along the rivers and coastal areas.

Thirdly, they grow into the yellow-brown eels that are usually spotted around ponds and lakes. They can spend whole seasons throughout the years hibernating in these places, often waking up when the pond they had been sleeping in dried up. And lastly, they become the strong, silvery and muscular eels we recognise the most. Once at their final stage, they use their powerful bodies to find their way back to the Sargasso Sea, the area where they were born. Found in the Bermuda Triangle, this sea has no land borders but is instead bordered by four separate currents (this is known as an ocean gyre).

During the fourth version's exhausting and long journey back to the ocean, their stomachs dissolve through the strain. After this, their reproductive organs develop for the first time in their lives.

By the time this happens, they are a long way from Europe, so we can now understand why the scientists in that part of the world could never find any eels with testicles (don't giggle, I told you!), as they hadn't developed yet!

Of course, we can understand this now because of modern science. But when poor Sigmund was elbow-deep in eel guts and trying to find something that wasn't there, we can probably forgive him for leaving zoology behind and concentrating on psychology!

Did you know?

The Bermuda Triangle is an area off the North Atlantic Ocean in which more than 50 ships and 20 airplanes have disappeared.

Fears of the Bermuda Triangle can be dated back to the 1800s, when ships which travelled through the area were found completely abandoned and others simply disappeard without a trace or even a distress call. Planes have been reported missing, and when rescue missions flew to the area, they also vanished. No wreckages were found.

While some believe that the disappearances are a result of supernatural activity (or that the Lost City of Atlantis lies beneath the ocean there!), the most generally accepted theory is that the environment is responsible.

The Bermuda Triangle is exposed to frequent hurricanes, tropical storms and rogue waves – humongous waves that reach up to 100 feet. It is certainly possible that these conditions could swallow up any ship that passed through.

Who Ran the First Marathon?

Before the marathon as we know it was ever an official race, a man named Pheidippides ran 24.22 miles to deliver a message before dropping dead moments after. Because of this, he unintentionally became the reason we have the world-famous race today.

Now, you may ask why he ran so far to bring a written note when he could have just sent a text, but you need to remember that back in 490 BC, mobile phones were not a thing. In fact, even the idea of such technology would have resulted in the person who suggested it being considered crazy. Of course, whether Pheidippides was a real person or just a legend created by the Greeks remains a mystery even today. Still, most historians believe he was genuinely alive in Ancient Greece and that he really did run 24.22 miles to deliver a message!

Being a 'runner' was a real job for certain soldiers throughout history, all the way up to World War I. The need to have someone who could get messages quickly and safely from the front lines back to the city was an essential part of any army. Those chosen to be runners were given intense stamina training, and it was considered a very noble job.

What we need to remember is that a lot of the details about the legend of Pheidippides have probably been stretched and changed over the years. Many more additions that certainly weren't true have surely been added over time, such as the version of this tale where he is meant to have run halfway around Greece without ever stopping!

But most believe that he did reach Athens from a little town called Marathon. And all to deliver the message that the Greek army had somehow defeated the mighty Persians.

If he died seconds later or not, we will probably never know. What we can say for sure is that the town of Marathon will forever be linked with the most famous race in the world. If legend is to be believed, and Pheidippides really did drop dead right after he handed over his note, then he could be forgiven for feeling a little annoyed that the race wasn't called a 'Pheidippides'! After all, he was the one who did all the running!

It would take nearly 2,500 years for the first official marathon to take place. This was in 1896, at the inaugural modern-day Olympics in Greece. It was to be a 24.22-mile race that was run in Athens. Now, isn't a marathon 26 miles long, I hear you ask? And you would be right to do so.

Yes, marathons today are actually 26 miles and 385 yards, to be exact. The gradual change in length happened as the Olympics switched countries every few years. The length of the race was constantly being changed slightly to suit whatever city it was in.

One such change came in London in 1908, when King Edward VII insisted that the distance be adjusted to ensure that the start line was situated directly outside his bedroom window. He made the people go to all this trouble just to make it possible for him to watch it without getting up.

Four years before King Edward's shocking show of laziness, the Olympics in St. Louis in America became something of a **farce** as the games began. In one event, gymnast George Eyser won six medals, including three gold. What made this already amazing achievement more impressive was that Mr Eyser did all of this with a wooden leg!

Something far more comical that happened at the 1904 games was in the marathon event when American runner Fred Lorz pulled a stunt that would have made Bugs Bunny proud. After taking off from the starter's pistol at full speed, Lorz began to suffer from stomach cramps not long after.

Running too fast at the start of a long race is something you should never do! Instead of pulling out of the race, he decided to hitch a ride. He slipped into one of the passing cars and then got dropped off near the finish line! He was caught just as he was about to receive his gold medal.

Some of the stranger events that have been part of the Olympic Games at different times throughout history include tug of war, ballooning, live pigeon shooting, and fine arts. The last of these saw participants receiving medals for things such as sculpting, painting, drawing, writing, and playing music!

So remember, the next time you want to get a message to someone who lives 24.22 miles away, send a text, make a call, or even do what Fred Lorz did and get a lift in someone's car!

Did you know?

Did you know that athletes in Ancient Greece used to compete in the nude? Gross, I know! But they did this to imitate the Gods and to clear toxins from their skin as they sweated. The word 'gymnastics' actually means 'to exercise naked' in Ancient Greek!

Not only were the men of Ancient Greek sometimes naked, they also wore skirts. They were seen as very manly back then and trousers were seen as women's clothing.

Have you ever heard the saying that gingers have no soul? Well, this likely stems from the beliefs of the Ancient Greeks. They used to think that redheads became vampires after they died – probably because redheads are paler than your average Mediterranean Greek and were therefore more sensitive to sunlight.

Who Fought the Shortest War in History?

Well, this question has a very clear answer. When we stack it up against the **Persian**-German War, which lasted 721 years, the **Anglo**-Zanzibar War of 1896 is like a grain of sand in the desert. Did it last a few years? No. Maybe it was several months? Guess again! No, the war between Britain and the tiny islands of Zanzibar lasted a whopping 38 minutes!

Back in 1890, the nation of Tanzania and the islands of Zanzibar had been split between Germany and Britain. The result of this treaty was that Zanzibar fell under the rule of the British Empire, and Tanzania now belonged to the Germans. Britain had several diplomats living in Zanzibar in the 19th century, but the British knew that they needed someone from Zanzibar in charge. This was done mostly for show.

Putting an Englishman as leader would likely have caused unrest and even riots among the locals. They decided to put a man named Hamad bin Thuwaini in charge, as he had previously been in favour of British rule. This way, they knew they could control him from the shadows and still keep the people of Zanzibar somewhat happy.

Sultan Hamad bin Thuwaini led Zanzibar through three years of peace until his untimely death in 1896. Although it has never been fully proven, it was always suspected that his cousin, Khalid bin Barghash, poisoned him. These rumours were pretty much confirmed when Khalid took the throne and surrounded the palace with his army barely minutes after the Sultan had passed away.

The British knew Khalid had murdered his cousin, and they ordered him to stand down. They wanted to hold another election and get another leader in charge who was loyal to Britain, but Khalid refused. Instead, he declared himself the new leader of Zanzibar, a move that angered the British.

Within days, the British had five warships lined up along the coast. Once there, they aimed all of their heavy artillery directly at the palace. Still, Khalid refused to surrender, and he ordered his tiny army of 3,000 soldiers to guard the palace at all costs.

The most powerful English diplomat in Zanzibar at the time was a man named Basil Cave. Under instructions from the government back in Britain and the head of the military, he was told to threaten Khalid with devastating action if he and his men didn't surrender. Khalid again sent word that they would never give up the palace and that he was indeed still the new ruler of his country.

The British gave Khalid one last chance to surrender, and when he refused, Rear Admiral Harry Lawson gave the warships the order to open fire. Within seconds, the palace was in flames, and the British sent in thousands of heavily armed men. Many of these soldiers were born in Zanzibar, and they were loyal to British rule.

Khalid's 3,000 men were barely armed, and the battle was quick and painful. Much of Khalid's army was killed, with the British only suffering one minor injury. The palace was reclaimed in 38 minutes as Khalid bin Barghash slipped away and found refuge at the German **consulate**. He lived out his days in exile in neighbouring Tanzania until he was found and arrested by British troops many years later during World War I.

War is never a good thing, but if it has to happen, then 38 minutes of fighting is a whole lot better than most. Khalid bin Barghash probably underestimated how the British would react and did so at his peril. It was this mistake that led to him becoming known as the man who started and fled the shortest war in history!

On the other end of the scale, the Dutch-Scilly War (sometimes referred to as The Three Hundred- and Thirty-Five-Years' War) lasted – you guessed it – 335 years! The length of this war can be blamed on miscommunication, as although the Dutch did in fact invade the Scilly Isles in 1651, they sailed home just 3 months later after being forced to surrender.

They had, however, forgotten to declare peace on the small Isles of Scilly before they left, so their conflict officially lasted until 1985, when a Scilly historian wrote to the Dutch Embassy to clarify this mishap. Whether or not this conflict can be called the longest in history is disputed by the fact that the Scilly Isles are not their own country (they're technically part of the United Kingdom), not a single shot was fired and not a single person died and well, because everyone had simply forgotten about it!

Have you ever heard of a country called Liechtenstein? This small, charming country (sixth smallest in the world) which is found between Switzerland and Austria may not be very well known, but there is one local war story which deserves a place in this book. Legend has it that during the Austro-Prussian War of 1866, 80 men left and 81 came back. Apparently the soldiers had nothing to do other than sit in the mountains and drink wine, so they returned with an Italian friend they had met along the way!

In 1932, Australia declared war on the most unlikely of creatures – emus! Large, flightless birds who were just minding their own business were targeted in the Great Emu War in an attempt to protect farmlands in Western Australia. Despite their efforts, the emu population prospered. Emus 1 – Australia 0.

Who Could Have Stopped the Black Death?

The world has had many terrible plagues and illnesses throughout history. All of them have been bad, but in the mid-1300s, the Black Death (or bubonic plague) was possibly the worst ever. When it was rapidly spreading through Europe and Asia, people genuinely worried that humanity could be fully wiped out.

In October of 1347, 12 ships arriving from voyages around the Black Sea docked at the Sicilian port of Messina. When the locals gathered at the dock to wait excitedly to see what spices and treasures the sailors had found on their travels, they had no idea of the horrors that awaited them on board.

As the boats were searched, they found that most of the sailors had already passed away or were very close to death. Their bodies were covered with huge boils—some the size of tennis balls—and their wounds were weeping blood and puss. Terrified, the locals forced the captains to leave with their ships, taking all on board with them. It was all too late though, and the disease had already spread to those on land. Soon a panic was gripping the whole continent of Europe as stories of the horrible plague from the Black Sea terrified everyone who heard them.

Around this time, Pope Gregory IX had been declaring that cats were the creation of the devil. He had his people instructing everyone who owned or spotted a cat to kill them at once. Now, I know that most people's opinions are split down the middle when it comes to cats. We either love them, or they give us the heebie-jeebies! But claiming that they should be sent back to hell would be an extreme reaction for even the biggest of cat haters!

But during the Middle Ages (generally accepted as between 500 and 1500 AD), superstitions were at their peak. Black magic, witchcraft, and spells were believed as fact. Those who were assumed to be practising such things were **ostracised** or, even worse, burned at the stake. Scary, I know!

Pope Gregory IX must have been a true believer in such stuff because he ordered all cats to be exterminated on sight. Unfortunately for the cats—and the world's population, it would turn out—most people listened. Very soon, Europe's cat population was at the lowest it had ever been.

Now, if you've heard of the Black Death before, you will know two things. One is that it devastated most of the planet, wiping out nearly one-third of the 60 million people who lived in Europe alone.

The second thing you might have heard is that, unlike most diseases that affect humans, this one was also spread by rats. Why is this second part so important in this little lesson? Well, let's just have a think about that for a moment!

What animal is known for being an expert hunter of rats? You guessed it! And what animal had the superstitious Pope Gregory IX ordered to be wiped out across Europe? You got it again!

Yes, many historians and scientists alike agree that if the cat population had not been decimated in the years leading up to the bubonic plague, then many of the rats which spread it would have been killed before they could.

Now, what if the cats who killed the rats (hey, I'm a poet, who knew!) ended up getting the disease too, you might ask? Well, much research has been done on this part of history, and the findings are much like people's views on cats—they are split down the middle. Half of those doing the research believe the cats would have just carried the disease in place of the rats. The other half think they would have stopped much of the plague from happening.

Whatever the case may be, I'm pretty sure that we can all agree that we would rather have the cats around at a time like that! As devastating of a mistake this was, 14th century Europe weren't the last to make such a blunder...

China in the 1950's was going through a transformation. To develop from an agrarian society (think farming and crops) to an industrial one (think lots of machinery, technology and big buildings), changes in every aspect of life had to be made. The animal kingdom was no exception. In 1958, a campaign was introduced to reduce the population of sparrows because they were eating the grains and seeds meant for the people.

The campaign was in full-swing when scientists started to realise their mistake. The sparrow population was near extinction, and they no longer ate the crops. However, they also no longer ate insects. With no predator around to curb the population, locusts swarmed the fields and farms and ate far more crops than the sparrows ever did.

The Chinese government even tried to import sparrows to fix the problem, but it was too late. The eradication of sparrows played a huge role in the Great Chinese Famine, in which 30 million people died of starvation.

May this chapter teach you a stark lesson:

Don't mess with Mother Nature!

Did you know?

> On the other hand, the Ancient Egyptians believed that cats were magical creatures who brought good luck, and they honoured and worshipped them with jewels and luxurious treats. When a cat died, their owner would shave off their eyebrow as a sign of mourning, and they would continue to mourn until they grew back. If anyone killed a cat, even by accident, they would be sentenced to death.

> In the Roman Empire, ferrets, dogs and monkeys were the most popular pets. They used the ferrets to hunt mice and rat, dogs as guards and monkeys as entertainment.

> In Ancient China, the favoured pet of the Emperors was the cricket! Initially, they liked the small insect for its song, but soon they began training them to fight each other for entertainment.

Who Is the Richest Person in History?

Is it Bill Gates? Elon Musk? Surely it has to be Jeff Bezos? No, the richest person in history was born in the 1300s in Mali, a country in West Africa. His name was Mansa Musa, and he was the ninth Mansa of the Mali Empire, which at the time controlled and occupied modern-day Senegal, Guinea, Mauritania, Gambia, and of course, Mali itself.

He was born at a time when Europe was in turmoil (the Black Death was nearing its beginning), and most African countries were booming. Gold and salt were plentiful, with salt then being far more rare and expensive than it is today. Throughout his life, Mansa Musa would become known for his generosity, and his lavish spending was often done for the good of the nation and the poor.

During his 25-year reign, the African leader would become known as the "King of Kings." Stories of his wealth spread across the entire globe. Once in power, he expanded the Mali Empire even further, giving special attention to the city of Timbuktu. (Yes, it is a real place!) There he had many universities, schools, mosques, and libraries. Soon, Timbuktu became known as the cultural centre of the world, much like Alexandria before and Paris after.

Now, we need to remember that while Europe's leaders were telling the people who lived there to kill their cats as the bubonic plague spread, Mali was becoming a place of magnificent wonders, knowledge, and sharing. Mansa Musa believed in spreading his wealth, and on a year-long **pilgrimage** to Mecca, tales of his generosity became the stuff of legend.

For his trip to Saudi Arabia and his eventual destination of Mecca, Mansa Musa's caravan (a large group of people travelling together, not a house on wheels!) was said to have been visible for miles before it even arrived. Those who witnessed it claimed that it contained 40,000 soldiers, thousands of camels, families carrying gold bars, and an endless line of helpers.

One of his most famous visits happened when he and his caravan stopped off in the bustling city of Cairo, Egypt. Now, the pharaohs of Egypt would have considered themselves to be the wealthiest people in the world. But the story goes that upon seeing Mansa Musa arrive with his massive supply of gold, salt, silks, and spices, the leaders of Egypt knew they could never compete with such riches.

Instead of buying everything he wanted for himself, Mansa Musa spread his money around, snapping up trinkets and souvenirs far above the set price and even handing out gold nuggets to beggars on the streets. All of this led to his reputation spreading all through Europe and Asia as well as the rest of Africa. After a while, his legend became so grand that he could not possibly live up to it.

His trip to Mecca lasted a whole year, and upon his return to Mali, he added even more schools and universities to the city of Timbuktu and many other places. Also, as a proud Muslim, he set to trying to bring all Muslim countries together, especially the Mamluk Empire (Egypt) and the Marinid Empire (Morocco).

Mansa Musa's time of death is still unknown, but historians believe it was probably around 1337. What we do know is that by the time of his passing, it was said that it would take a person atop a camel over four months to travel from one side of his empire to the other.

Of course, it was his astonishing wealth that he will always be remembered for. But we must never forget the generosity he showed throughout his reign as the King of Kings. Far too often, those who have become rich throughout history have spent their fortune selfishly, leaving those who struggle for income to only watch on in envy.

Many of the buildings and mosques he commissioned to be built are still standing today, almost 700 years later, including the wonderful Djinguereber Mosque in Timbuktu (I told you it was a real place!). Many scholars believe that the techniques used by the Mali builders in the 14th century laid the groundwork for all that we see in modern architecture today, which is truly amazing!

So the next time someone tells you that Elon Musk, Jeff Bezos, or even Bill Gates are the richest people in history, smile, let them speak, and then tell them nicely that it was, in fact, none of them.

It was a generous and revolutionary man named Mansa Musa who is the only person in history who can make that particular claim!

While the richest people alive today may not have the wealth of Mansa Musa, their fortune is still unimaginable. To put it into perspective the difference between a millionaire and billionaire, a million seconds a roughly 11.5 days, whereas one billion seconds is more than 31 years!

As of June 2022, there are 2668 billionaires in the world with a combined worth of $10 trillion dollars. Their wealth is greater than the combined wealth of 60% of the world's population. It is near impossible to accumulate this type of wealth: if you saved $10,000 every day since the building of the pyramids in Ancient Egypt, you would only have a fifth of the average fortune of the world's five richest billionaires.

The US has the world's most billionaires, with China following closely behind. While the COVID-19 pandemic was devastating for millions of people and economies worldwide, it was a breeding ground for new billionaires. Billionaires' wealth rose more in the first 24 months of the pandemic than in the last 23 years. The charity Oxfam estimates that the pandemic created a new billionaire every 30 hours!

Did you know?

Jeff Bezos (the founder of Amazon) has a greater GDP than Iceland, Afghanistan and Costa Rica combined.

It is estimated that he earns around $150,000 every minute! That's more than the average American earns in a year!

To put the wealth of a billionaire into perspective in what you could buy today (in dollars, because the most billionaires are in America), let's compare the relative prices for someone with the average household net worth versus the average billionaire net worth (a net worth is the value of everything you own).

The average American has a net worth of $121,000 and the average billionaire has a net worth of $2 billion. Therefore, the equivalent of $1 for the average American feels the same as $16,528 for the average billionaire.

So, for an average person in the States, a home costs $374,900, which of course is a lot of money. But because a billionaire has so much wealth, the prices do not feel the same, and this huge number only feels like $22.60.

People may save for years to buy a brand new $499 PlayStation 5, but to a billionaire, buying one is like dropping 3 cents in the street!

When you're on a flight and your legs are cramped and the food is terrible, you may look over in envy at those in first-class with a comfy, makeshift bed and all the fizzy drinks they like. The $10,000 price tag may seem ridiculous for these small comforts, but to a billionaire that only feels like 60 cents.

For us normal people, a brand new, luxurious car at $110,000 (a Range Rover to be specific) is an extravagance we simply cannot justify spending. But for billionaires, that's only $6.60. That's the price of a McDonalds!

38

Who Introduced Hippos to Colombia?

Once upon a time, there was a man named Pablo Escobar, and he was a nasty piece of work. We don't need to go into why here, but he was also extremely rich. This was how he was able to ship over four hippos for his own private zoo in the 1980s. What is strange about this story is that hippopotamuses were not native to Columbia. In fact, there weren't any at all in the wild there before this story takes place.

In 1993, Pablo Escobar was killed by the Colombian police. Upon his death, his unbelievably large ranch in the Columbian countryside went unattended for several years. During this time, the animals he kept—including giraffes, zebras, and flamingos—ran free across his land. Some of them were relocated to animal shelters after the ranch closed. Some went to other zoos, but the hippos were never found.

That was until they started to reproduce. Within a decade, almost 130 of them began to show up in the nearby town of Puerto Triunfo. Many zoologists believe that this number will keep increasing as the herd grows in size. They guess that the number could be as high as 400 hippos in as little as six years!

Although hippos are the third largest mammal, they are also herbivores, meaning they only eat fruit and vegetables, which seems strange given their massive size. But we must remember that most of the largest land animals on the planet are vegetarians. So the next time your parents tell you to eat your broccoli, make sure you do if you want to be as strong as the Rock!

Pablo Escobar's fortune and his property ended up meaning nothing once he was caught. All of his money and land were gained illegally, including his personal zoo.

Despite the fact that hippos were not **indigenous** to Colombia, the climate there was so similar to their natural one that it was easy enough for them to adapt. The same plants and shrubs that they eat were there. The water was the same temperature, and everything else they needed to prosper seemed to have been provided by nature, meaning that Colombia is now home to its very own population of hippos!

Did you know?

> Lord Byron, one of the greatest English poets of all time, once had a pet bear. In defiance of the rules at Cambridge stating that dogs were not allowed, he purchased a tame bear at a fair, and later brought it home to roam the grounds with his pet wolf. Years later, another iconic poet, Percy Shelley, wrote in his diary after visiting Byron's home that he had ten horses, eight dogs, three monkeys, five cats, an eagle, a crow and a falcon!

> Andrew Jackson, the 7th president of the United States, had a pet parrot (an African Grey) who was so grief-stricken after the passing of his owner, he had to be removed from the former president's funeral for swearing too loudly and disturbing the other attendees!

Who Was the Only Person Both a Dwarf and a Giant?

How could someone be both a dwarf and a giant? It seems impossible, right? Well, the case of Adam Rainer is pretty much as close to impossible as you can get. The man from Graz, Austria-Hungary, was recorded as both a dwarf and giant in his adult life. This means he is the only known person in history to be confirmed as both a dwarf and a giant!

Adam Rainer was born in 1899 to two parents of average height. As a youth, he was described as sickly and weak.

Nobody who knew him then would have believed that one day he would be declared a giant. Even into his teen years, Adam showed no signs of a growth spurt, although doctors at the time did note that he had surprisingly large hands and feet. At the age of 17 and with World War I raging all across Europe, young Adam tried to enlist in the army to help fight for his nation. Unfortunately, at just under four feet tall, he was officially declared too small to join up.

It was around this time that he was medically confirmed as a dwarf. Sad and dejected, Adam returned home to Graz.

Even with his short stature, Adam's shoe size was UK 10 (US 10.5), which would be considered typical for any male of average height. His hands also continued to grow much faster than his body, making his teen and early adult life rough. People can be cruel, and Adam Rainer had to grow up with a thick skin.

Usually, most human beings will stop growing at age 21. Even by the time they are 18 or 19 years old, their growth will have drastically slowed down. It seemed that by 1920, Adam Rainer's body decided to go the other way! During his next visit to the local doctor, at the age of around 21, his shoe size was recorded to have doubled, making it a whopping UK 20 (US 21). Also, his height had finally begun to catch up, and Adam started growing at a rate of 9.14 cm (3.16 inches) per year!

Over the next decade, Adam's growth would astound medics. When he had reached a height of seven foot two inches by the age of 33, he was sent to Vienna to see two of the best doctors in Europe. They discovered a benign tumour at the base of his brain and decided that this had most certainly been the reason for his incredible growth.

Now that Adam Rainer had been officially diagnosed, the doctors knew what they were dealing with. Plans were made to operate on the tumour. Around this time, he was also officially registered as a giant, making him the first and, thus far, the only person in history to be both a dwarf and a giant.

The doctors removed the tumour (through his nose!), but by that stage, Adam's body had already become weak through the physical strain of his rapid growth. His joints and muscles were not equipped for such drastic changes. According to medical reports, he lived a lot of his later life in severe pain.

Along with the agony he must have had to endure daily, his spine had started to curve to the side under the added weight, and Adam spent a lot of his time in a wheelchair. The removal of the tumour slowed his growth a little but didn't stop it. He passed away in 1950 at the age of 51. At the time, Adam Rainer was seven foot eight inches tall.

We know now that he suffered from acromegaly, a disorder that affects the growth hormone, causing it to react erratically. Many people today are diagnosed with this condition, and modern medical procedures can slow it down or even stop it if it is caught early enough.

Unfortunately for Adam Rainer, he was born at a time when research on such a disorder was almost non-existent. Despite all of this, he is said to have always carried himself with dignity, and he never once let his disability hold him back from leading a full life. The stories that remain of the man who was born a dwarf and died a giant paint a picture of someone who always tried to live with a smile on his face despite his hardships.

I like to think it was this brave and wonderful aspect of his personality that made him a true giant!

Did you know?

> The world's shortest woman, Jyoti Amge from India, is only 2 feet tall at 28 years old. That's half the height of Adam Rainer at his smallest!

> The world's tallest man is 8 feet and 2.8 inches - only 7 inches taller than Adam at his tallest.

The country you are from influences your height. I know it seems crazy, but it's true. Researchers have tracked the heights of populations for decades and the average height in one corner of the globe can be drastically different to another.

While Adam Rainer's short stature was very obvious in Europe, there are many places around the world where he wouldn't have been *that* much shorter than the average person.

The country with the shortest population in the world is Timor-Leste, an island in South East Asia. The average Timorese man is 5 ft. 2.9 inches and the average Timorese woman is 4 ft. 11.5 inches.

Compare that to the tallest country, The Netherlands in western Europe, where the average man is 6 ft. tall and the average woman is 5 ft. 6!

The next shortest countries are:

Laos in South East Asia – 5 ft. 1.37
Madagascar in Africa -5 ft. 1.56
Guatemala in Central America – 5 ft. 1.57
The Philippines in South East Asia – 5 ft. 1.57

The next tallest counties are:

Montenegro, a Balkan country in Southeast Europe– 6 ft
Denmark in Northern Europe – 5 ft. 11.9
Norway in Northern Europe – 5 ft. 11.8
Serbia, a Balkan country in Southeast Europe – 5 ft. 10.9

As you can see, the shortest populations are in developing countries and the tallest are in more **affluent** ones. The difference in height can be partly due to genetics and partly due to environment: people in developing countries are poorer and therefore more likely to be malnourished.

People in Europe have more access to a healthy diet and can therefore consume all the vitamins and nutrients needed to grow tall (that means eat your fruit and vegetables!). As a species, we are much taller and live much longer than ever!

Who Was the Real Cleopatra?

Most, if not all of us, have heard about Cleopatra in some form or another. She was the great leader of Egypt, famed for her cunning, intelligence, and beauty. Her reign was filled with both **controversy** and greatness. She has probably been brought to life in more television, books, and plays than any other person in history. We all know about her leadership skills and romantic relationships with Julius Caesar and Mark Antony, but who was the real Cleopatra?

Born in 69 BC, she was the daughter of King Ptolemy XII Auletes. Her parents were actually Macedonian and not Egyptian. Still, Cleopatra was born in Egypt, and her distant relatives were all considered Egyptian royalty, making her rise to the throne in later life a little more understandable. Of course, all of her achievements came through her own intelligence and determination.

When Cleopatra's father died, she was 18. Since she was female, the throne was passed on to her younger brother, Ptolemy XIII. Can you imagine her brother was given power when he was only 10 years old! But he was too young to realistically rule, and historians believe that all of the decisions made during this period were done so by the king's older sister, Cleopatra.

Now, this is the part of the story where things get a bit strange (icky even!), so prepare yourself! Historians are nearly sure that Cleopatra soon married Ptolemy (eww, I told you it got icky!). After a few years together, her younger brother (and husband!) started to show signs of jealousy and anger toward her. Knowing that all of his followers were aware that Cleopatra was really running the country, Ptolemy XIII let his emotions get the better of him, and he banished her from Egypt forever.

Of course, Cleopatra was not one to slink away into the night without a fight. Instead, she returned to Egypt soon after and, with the help of Julius Caesar and a large chunk of the Roman Army, defeated her brother in battle. He was drowned in the Nile River, and Cleopatra became an Egyptian royal again.

She wasn't done there, though, and not long after the death of her husband (and brother, double eww!), she married another brother, Ptolemy XIV (triple eww). After all of this controversy, we might think that things would settle down for a while, right? Wrong. Soon after her second marriage, it is understood that Cleopatra ordered the **assassination** of Ptolemy XIV. Nothing could stop her as she continued to do everything to have the throne all to herself.

But she also had a sister, Arsinoe, who could legally take charge of the country if Cleopatra ended up with no brothers (which seemed likely after all the murders!). Maybe young Cleo would have had enough of killing her siblings, I hear you say. Perhaps it was only brothers she wanted out of the way as they would always get the throne ahead of her? Nope. Historians believe that Cleopatra had Arsinoe killed too!

But it is far too easy to get caught up in the dramatic parts of Cleopatra's life. We also need to understand that when she used her beauty to get what she wanted, it was often the only option she had. Throughout history, women were not given much of a chance to rule. For someone in her position to rise up to the heights she did, it would have taken more than a coy smile and flapping eyelashes! It took guts and leadership.

Cleopatra was brilliant, and her intelligence was her strongest asset. Apart from the 12 different languages she could speak, she was highly educated in mathematics, **oratory**, astronomy, and philosophy. Some historians even go so far as to claim that her beauty was partly myth, and it was actually her brilliance and a magnetic charm that made her irresistible to all who met her.

Cleopatra died at the age of 39. Although we know it was poison that killed her, we will probably never be sure if it was suicide, murder, or a snake bite. Whatever way it happened, she will be forever known as one of the greatest leaders of all time. And she was the last true ruler of Egypt before it was swallowed up by the Roman Empire.

Did you know?

I know we associate Cleopatra with Ancient Egypt and Ancient Egypt with the Pyramids of Giza, but did you know that Cleopatra was born closer in time to the building of the first McDonald's than to the building of the pyramids? The construction of the pyramids took place from 2550 BC to 2490 BC, while Cleopatra was born in 69 BC and died in 30 BC. That's a difference of 2,460 years. The first McDonald's opened in California in 1955, which was 1,984 years after Cleopatra was born. So, not only was she born closer to the opening of McDonald's, but it was 476 years closer!

Who Were the Other Species of Human?

Living comfortably in the 21st century, it may be unimaginable that once, us humans were not at the top of the food chain. In fact, we weren't even close. Our prehistoric ancestors spent their whole lives fighting for survival, as they hunted, gathered and skillfully navigated the everchanging climate and terrain of the Earth. From the scarcity of the Ice Age to the plains of the Stone Age, humans managed to adapt to their surroundings and overcome the predators and the disease to lead to us to where we are today.

While you may think it seems unlikely that humans would survive such unlikely conditions, what if I told you that many of us actually didn't? In prehistoric times, there were at least a dozen other species of human which either predated us or lived alongside us. None of them could survive these challenges and now we are the only ones left.

When we think of cavemen, you may have once thought that one phase of evolution led to another, which led to another, which led to another. And while this is true (for evolution most definitely requires the process of evolving) there were also other branches of humans which stemmed off from the progression of humans which we are familiar with today. All these different prehistoric humans looked slightly different, had different skillsets and occupied different landscapes. There are 21 recognised human species, but some sources only list 10-12 of these as 'human'. Here are some biographies of some notable species of human...

Homo Sapiens (us!)

Latin meaning: Wise man
First dates back around 200,000 years ago.
Location: East Africa*
Known for: large, complex brains which allowed us to create more advanced tools and complicated language skills. Our primitive curiosity has greatly contributed to the studies of science, philosophy and mythology.

We also have less developed jaws and smaller teeth than our prehistoric brothers and sisters. It is believed that this directly led to our intelligence, because smaller teeth meant more room in our skulls for our brain to grow!

And how did our teeth evolve to be smaller, you ask? Through the discovery of fire! By cooking our food, we no longer needed strong jaws to chew. I know, evolution is a marvelous phenomenon.

We are also a highly social species. Our ancestors created communities amongst each other in ways that other species of humans didn't. This is believed to be another factor which helped us survive when others didn't.

*some **paleontologists** believe it is North Africa

Homo Habilis

Latin meaning: Handy man

They lived between 2.4 to 1.5 million years ago.

Location: sub-Saharan Africa

Known for: being the first toolmaker. Their invention of tools allowed them to kill large animals and have access to new sources of protein, which paved the way for all meat-eating humans (even you!). The Homo habilis were one of the earliest types of humans. Although they also had a larger brain and smaller teeth (which made them stand out from other apes) they still had some ape-like features, such as long arms.

Homo Erectus/ Ergaster

Latin meaning: Upright man

They lived between 1.89 million years ago until about 110,000 years ago.

Location: Northern, Eastern and Southern Africa as well as Western & East Asia.

Known for: being the first humans to migrate out of Africa, discovering fire and being able to run for long distances. They have survived on the earth far longer than any other human species.

The Homo erectus are the oldest known early humans. With longer legs and shorter arms, this species of human are thought to be the first to live on the ground instead of in the trees and are believed to be extremely fast to evade predators on the ground. They lived on the earth 9 times longer than our own species has existed.

To put these dates into perspective, civilisation as we know it is only 6,000 years old and the internet is only 40 years old!

Homo Floresiensis

Nickname: The hobbits

They lived between 100,000 – 50,000 years ago.

Location: Indonesia

Known for: being real life hobbits! They were around 3 foot 6 in height as an adult and had small brains, large teeth and large feet.

The size of the Homo floresiensis is believed by scientists to be something called 'island dwarfism'. This is a long evolutionary process which results from their species being isolated on an island. Remember how we discussed that evolution changes our bodies so that we can survive? Well, with island dwarfism, the Homo floresiensis likely became smaller and smaller over tens of thousands of years so that they could survive with less food, because there was less food available to them. Smart, right? Despite their small size, they are thought to have used tools and captured predators.

Homo Neanderthalensis

Name meaning: named after the Neander Valley in Germany, which is where their fossils were first discovered.

They lived between 200,000 years ago and 35,000 years ago.

Location: Eurasia – scientists believe they inhabited all the way across the world from present-day Belgium, down to the Mediterranean and through southwest Asia.

Known for: their strength. Despite the fact that they were shorter than the average human, they are believed to have been much stronger. When you think of a typical caveman, the Neanderthal is probably the one you think of. This is because Neanderthals lived in caves of limestone, which preserved their bones well and meant that scientists were able to figure out a lot of information about them.

There is an air of mystery surrounding the extinction of the Neanderthals. Scientists believe that they died out around 40,000 years ago, after a wave of Homo sapiens (us) migrated out of Africa around 20,000 years earlier. It is clear that our ancestors encountered and interacted with Neanderthals, because some people have a tiny bit of Neanderthal DNA! Whether or not our ancestors had anything to do with the extinction of the Neanderthals is unclear. Other explanations for their extinction include natural disasters, such as volcanic eruptions, or failure to adapt to changes in climate.

Did you know?

> Unicorns once existed. The Siberian Unicorn (or Elasmotherium sibiricum) was an Ice Age giant and ancient ancestor of the Rhino which lived in present-day Kazakhstan. Their huge, single horn in the centre of their forehead may be the inspiration for the legends of unicorns in mythology.

> When you think of the Sahara Desert, you probably think of barren sand dunes and camels. But did you know that 100 million years ago (when dinosaurs ruled the earth), the Sahara Desert was inhabited by ginormous crocodiles? Back then, the landscape was a lush swampland, and these ancient crocs had both their usual croc-abilities (such as swimming) as well as legs which made them very agile runners. Some of the croc species could grow up to 40-feet long, and instead of hunting antelope and deer like today's crocodiles, they hunted dinosaurs.

Who Were the Rock Stars of the Roman Empire?

Although most gladiators were originally slaves or criminals, once they had won a few fights in the Colosseum or the other smaller arenas, they would often become quite the celebrities around Rome. They were seen the same way rock stars or sports stars are today, and their lives outside of the arena could be one that was considered pretty glamorous.

Of course, not all gladiators lived this way. Only the elite few who won over the crowds became celebrated and loved. But when they did, they became irresistible to the ladies who would scream and faint as they entered the Colosseum. Also, all of the young boys who were there dreamed of one day being just like their favourite gladiator.

Now, we have to remember that apart from these rare times when a gladiator rose above his expected place in life, they were seen as lower class, slaves, and even someone else's property. Yes, you read that last part correctly. A gladiator was actually the property of the wealthy person who bought or trained them from their youth.

You see, owning a gladiator wasn't cheap, as they had to be housed, fed, and trained. When a rich or noble person owned a gladiator, they would usually have several, so they would need a large building where they could all live and sleep. On top of that, the gladiators were muscular and strong like modern-day wrestlers, so they needed plenty of food to keep them in shape.

One of the strange things about their eating habits is that according to recent studies of gladiator remains, most of them appeared to be vegetarian! That might not seem so strange in today's world, but 2,000 years ago, vegetarianism was almost seen as black magic. Recent research done on the bones of 67 gladiators showed scientists that the majority of them had lived on a plant-based diet with little animal protein.

We know from our earlier lesson that the three largest land mammals on the planet are vegetarian, so maybe a load of muscle-bound gladiators gulping down bowl after bowl of beans isn't such a strange thought after all!

When we picture gladiators, we will often imagine them walking out into the middle of a sun-drenched Colosseum to the screams and shouts of thousands of spectators. This is most often how it was. When the gladiators reached a certain height of their fame, they became the rock stars of Ancient Rome.

This was when things would get a little crazy for them. Clay toys depicting the most popular gladiators of the time were sold to children, who battled with them in front gardens and schoolyards all across Italy. Much like WWE or G.I. Joe figures, these models of the gladiators were popular among the kids.

Amazingly, those kids were allowed into the arenas to watch the blood and guts shows that were put on. I wonder if "arena time" was something parents argued about, as they do about screen time today!

Another strange thing that happened back then was that the sweat of the most famous gladiators became a **commodity**. That's right; their sweat! Even 2,000 years ago, people were self-conscious about their appearance. For the skin cream, salespeople would scrape the sweat off a gladiator after his match, bottle it, and sell it as the world's most incredible skin product! Lots of wealthy women bought these creams, and they were even seen as a delicacy.

Now, you might have heard that gladiators always fought till the death, but this has been a little twisted to suit Hollywood movies and Netflix shows. Yes, sometimes the matches would last until one of the fighters was dead. But more often than not, the fight was stopped before that happened. Remember that to house, feed, and train the gladiators, their owners had to spend an awful lot of money. They were hardly going to go through all those years of trouble and expense just to send their gladiator in for one match!

This was how the more popular gladiators were able to live for a long time, often making a lot of money themselves and earning their right to retire a free man. Of course, the life of a gladiator was excessive, and most of them probably didn't make it to old age. Still, while they were around, they had action figures made in their image, and all the girls wanted to kiss them, so things weren't all bad!

Did you know?

> The status of a gladiator was so well-respected and sought after that according to superstition, any boy who even dreamed of fighting a gladiator was destined to marry a beautiful woman.

When did Animals Have Jobs?

This chapter is going to start with the crazy story of Caligula: a once beloved Roman emperor whose power and great wealth turned him into a cruel and insane tyrant. He reigned over Ancient Rome between 37-41 AD, and in these four years he earned himself the title of one of the most outrageous leaders in history. He lived a life of luxury, and spent today's equivalent of millions on the finest silk robes, diamond headbands and expensive wigs to mimic the gods. Not only did he attempt to dress like them, he also insisted to anyone who would listen that he spoke to them often.

By drinking pearls and bathing in gold, he did everything he could to place himself above the mortals. To give him credit, it kind of worked. He got away with whatever he wanted. When he wanted to be the best gladiator or chariot racer in Rome, he fought in the Colosseum against those who were severely injured right before the match and raced against those who were instructed to lose or face death! He was a short and unattractive man, and insisted that taller people crouch when they spoke to him so he never had to look up to them. When he went bald in his early twenties, he even created the rule that nobody was allowed to look at the top of his head when he passed!

Now, his power as emperor allowed him to get away with the most ridiculous things, but the most ridiculous of all was when he made his favourite horse, Incitatus, a consul (the highest elected position in Ancient Rome, whose job is to command armies and oversee the Senate). Though this never came into fruition, as Caligula was killed before it became official, Incitatus still got to enjoy the luxuries a consul normally would, only in horse form! This included slaves (human), a marble stable, drinking wine with Caligula at the table and eating gold-studded oats. It's hilarious to imagine how Incitatus would have performed in his new job role, had Caligula not been murdered.

Now, while Caligula may have been a power-crazed bully, and Incitatus (bless him) was greatly underqualified for the job at hand, it got me thinking about other times throughout history when animals have been given jobs to benefit humans. I know we've all heard of guide dogs, sheep dogs or cats chasing mice, so let's take a deeper look at some examples you may have never heard of before or of examples where the animals are specifically trained for the job!

Execution by Elephant

While you've probably heard of the beheadings of the wives of Henry VIII in medieval England, or the countless women who were burnt at the stake during the Salem witch trials in the 17th century, did you know that in Ancient Asia, elephants were used as public executioners? This practice has been documented back to a time of empires and kingdoms, all the way up to the 19th century, when it stopped as a result of colonisation by the Europeans. Elephants were a symbol of power for nobles: if a royal could control such a huge, powerful creature, they were clearly fit to lead a kingdom. Though gentle and passive by nature, they were vigorously trained to crush prisoners on command, either because they had committed a terrible crime or simply for entertainment for the masses. In Siam (present-day Thailand), elephants were trained to throw the prisoner in the air before they were trampled to death!

License to Krill

Of course, there are police dogs used by the police-force, guide dogs used by the disabled and sheep dogs used by farmers, but guess which animals the military use? Dolphins and sea lions! The United States Navy created a programme in 1960 which trained marine animals to help them detect enemy swimmers during the Vietnam War. After testing more than 19 species, Bottlenose dolphins were chosen because of their impressive **echolocation** skills and California sea lions were chosen because of their impeccable underwater vision. There are five teams which train the animals in different areas: one team specialised in swimmer detection (so that the military are alert to enemies coming to attack by sea); three teams in mine location and one in object recoveries.

Baboonin' Around

In the late 1800's, a Chacma Baboon by the name of Jack was an official employee for a railway in South Africa. His owner, a man called James Wide, worked at the railway and was known for jumping between the railcars, until one day he fell and lost both of his legs. To adjust to his disability, James then found Jack the Baboon and trained him to help to push his wheelchair and to change the railway signals in 1881. James' employers were sceptical at first, but after witnessing Jack successfully pulling levers in response to the signal whistle at the station, they decided to officially employ him. He was paid 20 cents a day and a half a bottle of beer a week. In his 9 years as a signalman (or rather, as a signalbaboon), Jack never made a mistake!

Canary Alarms

If you have ever read The Hunger Games, you will definitely have heard of this one! A huge part of the British mining culture is their relationship with canaries – a small, bright yellow bird. Though the songbirds might seem out of place in the dark gloom of the mines, the canaries were companions of the miners for most of the 1900s because of their ability to detect dangerous gases. Carbon monoxide, a poisonous gas, was a real threat to miners because it was colourless and odourless. People don't realise they are breathing it in until it's too late. So, the miners would bring down a singing canary with them as they worked. Because of their small size, canaries are sensitive to the air. If the canaries stopped singing, the miners would know that something wasn't right and could quickly evacuate. Nowadays, we can use technology to detect the dangerous gases, but the image of the coalminer covered in soot gently holding a bright yellow songbird will be one that is forever remembered with this industry.

Who Stole Albert Einstein's Brain?

Before we try to answer this most ridiculous of questions, let's have a little back story on one of the most brilliant people in history. Albert Einstein was born in Germany in 1879. He showed intelligence at an early age and was studying at a secondary level even as a child. At the age of 12, young Albert taught himself algebra and geometry in the space of a single summer! His family's business went bankrupt in his teens, and his parents moved to Milan. Einstein, who was 15 by then, stayed in Germany to finish his studies before following them to Pavia that December.

He graduated from university at the age of 21 and soon after moved to Bern, Switzerland. There, he found himself restless—as is often the case with geniuses—and he took a pretty boring job in a patent office.

He continued to be a physicist, though and studied whenever he could. During this period, he spent his free time writing several books and theories. Four of them would be groundbreaking, and amazingly, all of them would be written in only one year. This particular year, 1905, has become known as Albert Einstein's "miracle year."

Of the four papers that would soon bring Einstein his first taste of fame, the most popular was on the theory of relativity (or $E=mc^2$, as it is often known). We could get into this now, but we would be here all year!

Einstein's wealth increased a little at this time, and he was able to dedicate much more time to his studies and theories. A decade later, he would publish what most scholars and historians believe to be his masterpiece. It was an expanded version of his theory of relativity, and it changed science forever. His calculations (far too technical for me to explain!) were proved 100% correct four years later by Sir Arthur Eddington during a solar eclipse in 1919.

After this, Albert Einstein became something like a celebrity, and his life would never be the same again. Luckily, the man famed for his vast intellect was also someone who could laugh at himself. His humour became a big part of the person we remember today, and it helped him to deal with his new life in the public eye.

In 1921 he won the Nobel prize for his services to physics, and a year later, he visited America for the first time. He continued to travel all over the world over the the next decade, giving talks at universities and colleges in many different countries.

But when World War II broke out in his native Germany, Albert Einstein was forced to flee Europe and move to the United States to save himself and his family from persecution. In the United States, he found a country that adored him for who he was, and Albert settled there and lived out the rest of his days. Amazingly, at the grand old age of 73, he was asked by the government of Israel to become their next president. Einstein turned the position down, but he was deeply moved that such an important job had been offered to him.

He died three years later in the University Medical Centre of Princeton, New Jersey, the city where he had moved to during the war two decades before.

After his death, his brain was removed and preserved under the agreement of his family in the hopes that future science could figure out what made him so intelligent. And that finally brings us to our original question: Who stole Albert Einstein's brain?

Now, when I mentioned that Einstein's family had given permission for the doctor to remove his brain, that might have been stretching it a bit. In reality, a man named Dr Thomas Harvey, who was performing the autopsy, illegally removed the brain (and the eyeballs!) without the family knowing. Einstein's son, Hans Albert Einstein, didn't find out what had happened until after his father had been cremated a few days later.

Surprisingly, Hans still agreed to allow Dr Harvey to keep the brain, but only if he published his findings in medical journals for the world to study. Dr Harvey agreed, and he swore to anyone that would listen that he only did what he did for the good of science. Of course, that became harder to believe as time went on. Dr Harvey even went so far as to travel around America with the preserved brain in a jar and sell pieces of it to other curious researchers. He photographed it endlessly and even commissioned an artist to paint a picture of it. All of Dr Harvey's games caught up with him, and he soon lost his job at Princeton University. On top of that, he lost his medical licence, meaning he could never be a doctor again. Also, due to the stresses and non-stop pressure of journalists and the public, his wife left him too.

Einstein's brain did end up being somewhat properly studied decades later, with mixed and unclear results. It turns out that we know little to nothing about how our brains really work, and considering Thomas Harvey was keeping what was left of Albert Einstein's brain in a jar locked inside a cooler for 40 years, we can assume that it wasn't very easy to study, anyhow.

But when you remember Albert Einstein, think of a man whose work and theories paved the way for the inventions of satellites, lasers, and mobile phones, among many other things! It was not only his brain which made him one of the most impressive men of all time, but it was also how he handled the recognition he recieved for being so intelligent.

Not only was Albert Einstein an intellectual genius, his activism for civil rights throughout his lifetime proved him to be a man of true integrity. He experienced anti-Semitism as a Jewish scientist in Germany under Hitler's rule, and although he fled the country in 1933, he continued to help those that could not leave by convincing world leaders (such as Winston Churchill) to help other Jewish scientists escape and then employ them in their respective countries, therefore saving thousands of lives.

He continued to be outspoken in the face of injustice in the United States. Racism towards African Americans was very common and generally accepted in this time, but Einstein openly condemned these attitudes, calling it a 'disease'.

When the first black American to earn a PhD from Harvard University was wrongfully arrested, Einstein volunteered to come to the trial and vouch that he was a good person! After Einstein had used his fame to make people aware of the injustice, the judge immediately dropped the case.

Einstein recognised his power as a famous and well-respected man and used it for good. He was a man of true honour and a great example of how to use your power for good!

Did you know?

There are more synapses (nerve connections) in your brain than there are stars in the galaxy! Astronomers estimate that there are more than 200 billion stars in the Milky Way. But **neuroscientists** estimate that the number of synapses in the average 3-year-old is around 1 quadrillion. As we grow older, a refining process occurs and we are left with half that many (still about 500 trillion synapses).

Who Could Predict the Future?

Well, someone actually predicting the future is impossible, so that heading might have been a bit misleading. But the odd time, a person in history has said or written something that has eerily come to pass. There are those who will point to someone like Nostradamus and claim that he could see into the future, sure. But he was the same as any fortune teller who works in a stall at a travelling circus. All they do is give broad answers that can be taken to mean anything at all.

Usually, the person listening to these predictions wants to hear a certain thing, so they will do everything they can to agree with what is being predicted. I mean, who doesn't want to be told they'll make a fortune in two years or that a tall, handsome stranger will fall in love with them? But true fortune telling and predictions are reserved for movies and comics. All of this isn't to say that some people haven't gotten close, though. And when I asked who could predict the future, you might be shocked to hear that we have two answers!

The first comes from a man named Edgar Allan Poe:

Edgar Poe was born in 1809 in Boston, Massachusetts. His father left the family not long after, and his mother died when he was two years old. He was fostered by a new family, and 'Allan' was added to his name. His childhood was both showered with generosity and also severe strictness, and by the time he was 13, young Edgar Poe was already writing constantly.

This lasted for the rest of his life, and in 1840, he released a collection of short stories. Most of them were in genres that had never been popular before that time, namely horror. Other stories in the collection are credited with creating the genre of detective fiction, and Poe is widely considered the father of the detective novel.

But it is his darker stories he is famous for, with the most popular being his 1845 poem - The Raven. The tale of an unnamed man slipping into madness as he chats with a talking raven (or does he?!) is scary stuff. It shot Edgar Allan Poe to fame, and it is still popular nearly two centuries later. Maybe you have seen the first-ever Simpsons "Halloween Special" when they retell the story? Even in cartoon form, it is creepy!

Unfortunately, Edgar Allan Poe didn't get to enjoy much of his newfound celebrity, and he died in 1849 at the age of 40 in (you guessed it) mysterious circumstances.

But we are here to talk about his eerie prediction, right? Well, Edgar Allan Poe never claimed that his novel The Narrative of Arthur Gordon Pym of Nantucket (long name for a book, huh?) was a glimpse into the future. But the similarities of what would occur later on in real life are strange, to say the least.

In the book, four crew members on a whaling ship become lost at sea when their boat capsizes. Hungry and scared, they soon find themselves coming close to madness and death. In a desperate attempt to stay alive, they draw lots to see which one of them shall be killed and eaten by the rest! As the tale goes, the youngest crew member pulls the shortest straw and is the one who becomes dinner! The character is a young cabin boy, and he ends up being eaten by the other three! His name? Richard Parker.

Fast forward 46 years, and a boat travelling from London to Sydney, Australia, capsizes halfway there. The crew, (you guessed it) hungry and scared, and (yep, got it again) close to madness and death, draw lots to see who should be killed and eaten to save the rest.

Now, if that wasn't bizarre enough, then there is an extra point for guessing the name of the poor unfortunate crew member who drew the short straw?

Did you pick Richard Parker? Or would that just be too insane? Well, it was the youngest member on the boat, and yes, his name actually was Richard Parker!

The second of our strange predictions comes from an author who was not nearly as famous as Edgar Allan Poe, but his story is just as crazy. His name was Morgan Robertson, and he wrote hundreds of short stories and novels, almost all about boats and the sea.

One of his most popular books, Futility (often called The Wreck of the Titan), is so similar to the sinking of the real Titanic that it is almost impossible to fathom. For one thing, the boat in Robertson's story is called the Titan, which is only two letters away from the Titanic. In the book, the ship is told to be 'unsinkable,' which was, of course, the big selling point of the Titanic.

There are even more similarities, with some of the strangest ones being that both ships set sail from Britain. They were also both the biggest ships ever made. In fact, the measurements of the

Titan in the book are almost exactly the same as the Titanic. Robertson's tale also has the Titan with far too few lifeboats (the Titanic was the same). In one of the most insane coincidences, the boats in both book and reality were recorded as travelling at pretty much identical speeds when they crashed into (you guessed it) an iceberg.

You might be thinking that there are already more than enough similarities to make this something unexplainable, but there were more! Both ships sank on a cold April night, and both in the North Atlantic. And at the horrific end of each of the tales, most of the 2,500 souls on board died in the icy waters.

I think the strangest thing of all about Morgan Robertson's book about the Titan and the links it has to the Titanic is that the book was written over 14 years before the Titanic was even built! But even the author himself dismissed any suggestions that he could see into the future. When asked, he simply told his interviewer that he was very knowledgeable about boats and that he was just writing about what he knew. Still, even if predicting the future is not possible, Edgar Allan Poe and Morgan Robertson gave it a real good go!

Speaking of the Titanic and weird coincidences would not be complete without mentioning Violet Jessop. Violet was an Argentinian nurse who worked as a stewardess on board ships. In 1911, she worked on the RMS Olympic until it collided with a British warship. Everyone survived, but Violet was transferred onto the RMS Titanic... Amongst the chaos after the Titanic hit the iceberg, she was given a baby to look after and placed on a lifeboat. But that's not all. Having survived unscathed yet again, she was then placed on the HMHS Britannic. In 1916, the ship exploded in the ocean after hitting a deep sea mine. Jessop and other passengers were nearly killed while escaping as the ship's propellers shredded the lifeboats close to it. She had to jump out of the lifeboat, which resulted in a head injury. Nevertheless, she survived yet again! She really has earned the nickname of 'Miss Unsinkable'.

Did you know?

This next coincidence, though completely unplanned, creates an odd feeling of the full-circle-ness of life. World War I claimed an estimate one million British lives. Yet somehow, the first recorded casualty of the war, 17-year-old soldier John Parr, and the last recorded casualty, 30-year-old George Edwin Ellison, are buried next to each other. Their grave stones are a mere 15 feet apart and face each other in the Saint Symphorien Military Cemetery.

The science fiction novel, Stand on Zanzibar written by John Brunner in 1969, was set in 2010 (forty years in the future) and featured the first African-American president of the United States. What was his name, might you ask? President Obomi! John Brunner was only one year and one letter off predicting President Obama, who became president in 2009!

The odds of you being killed by a meteor are 1 in 1.6 million. After all, meteors could travel through space for billions of years without hitting anything at all, so the chance of it hitting you are miniscule. This information makes the next story even more peculiar. In 2011, a meteor which scientists estimate was 4.57 billion years old, fell through the Earth's atmosphere and smashed through the roof of a family home on the outskirts of Paris. Their name? The Comettes! This was not only a strange coincidence but also extremely unlikely, as only 50 meteorites had called in France in the last 400 years. The meteor itself was a piece of chondrite that had come from a belt of asteroids between Mars and Jupiter and is thought to be partly made of dust it has collected along the way, including dust which predates the formation of our very own solar system. Crazy, right?

What is the Grossest Story in History?

I know you may find the cough medicine your mother forces you to take absolutely rancid, but after reading this chapter, I bet you will thank your lucky stars that you were born in a time of modern medicine! It wasn't always as easy as going to the doctor and taking some tablets to cure illnesses. No, it took a while for humanity to get to this stage, and some of the methods they used in the past are just absolutely gross...

Like the fact that in Ancient Rome, instead of gargling with a minty fresh concoction, they used stale urine as mouthwash because urine contains ammonia, which can be used to clean. It was so commonplace to use urine that they actually had to pay a tax on it! Yuck!

Similarly, the Tudors used a mixture of poo and honey to remove rotten teeth! If they weren't rotten before, they definitely would be after that...

The Great Plague of London in the late 1600s was a ghastly illness which took 15% of the London population. People were desperate for a cure and would try anything. Some even believed that it could be cured by plucking the feathers from a live chicken and then strapping its bottom onto any affected areas!

Back in prehistoric times, cavemen used the most unlikely of animals to assist them during surgery. Ants! They would put an ant above an open wound and wait for it to bite the skin with its pincers. Once it had bitten them, they would remove the head and leave the pincers as a stitch.

Known as the 'father of medicine', Ancient Greek Hippocrates used to diagnose his patients by tasting their wee, ear wax and bogies! Yuck, I know, but without him maybe we would not understand medicine as we do today.

Though perhaps not as gross as the others, did you know that ketchup was first sold as medicine? In 1834, it was sold as a cure for an upset stomach in Ohio, and only became a popular condiment until decades later.

Let's move away from medicine now and talk about one part of history that is guranteed to be gross: toilets! Did you know that King Henry VIII of England was so powerful and rich that he had servants who were called 'Grooms of Stool', whose job it was to wipe his bottom after he went to the toilet! These Grooms of Stool were eventually knighted, but I'm still not sure it was worth it...

Normal people in these times didn't have their own bottom wipers, rather the opposite. They would sit on communal toilets and share a sponge on a stick to clean themselves!

In the sweltering heat of Ancient Egypt, Pharoah Pepi II was far too important to swat away the omnipresent flies. Instead, he would lather his slaves in honey to attract, trap and kill the flies. That's a much better story than simply having slaves fan them away!

In the Incan Empire (found in South America), they would worship llamas and sacrifice hundreds of them every month to appease their gods. They would then make bracelets out of the llama toenail clippings!

In the Stone Age, food was scarce and never wasted. If people were somehow able to kill a bear, they would then rip open its stomach to eat the meal that the bear had last eaten before it was killed! Gross! It's hard to pick the worse one, isn't it? I hope this chapter hasn't put you off your dinner!

Conclusion

I hope you have enjoyed your lessons on some weird and wacky aspects of our history. Maybe, in places, the stories made you smile, and hopefully, they also made you want to learn more. Remember that studying new things and filling yourself up with knowledge is one of the greatest gifts in the world. When we broaden our minds, we feel better inside, and that is something that should be cherished.

Even when it is something as bizarre as Sigmund Freud looking for eel testicles (don't laugh!) or books that seem to predict the future, it is all good stuff. If you manage to have a couple of laughs while learning new things, then all the better, right?

History is vitally important, as it lets us have a glimpse into the minds of those who lived it. Far too often, we can quickly judge someone for their actions in the past, but unless we understand what their world was actually like, then we don't really have the right to do so.

Every generation thinks and acts differently. This can be caused by their surroundings, their upbringing, or simply the fact that what we know now on the subject in question wasn't fully understood back then. Always remember that those in the future who look back on people in 2022 will probably think a lot of the stuff we said and did was crazy or silly. But that doesn't mean that it is. No, all it means is that we are constantly learning as we move forward.

Never be ashamed to learn new things, and please don't ever hide the fact that you want to. So keep on reading, and always do it with a smile on your face.

Thanks for learning with me!

Glossary

Affluent: Wealthy/rich

Anglo: Derived from the Latin word 'Anglia' which means England, this can refer to either the people or language descending from England

Assassination: The murder of an important person, usually for political reasons

Avid: Keen or eager

Bout: A wrestling or boxing match

Commodity: Something that is sold

Consulate: An building dedicated for the government representative of another country (similar to an embassy)

Controversy: A disagreement between lots of people with opposing views

Disband: Break up

Dynasty: A line of people from the same family who play an important role in a country, business or politics (& more!)

Echolocation: A way for dolphins and other marine life to 'see' but not with their eyes. They interpret the echoes of sound waves that bounce off objects around them in the water. When they produce a vibration through the water by making a clicking sound, the vibrations that bounce back to them will be different if there is a whale or just a small fish in front of them

Glossary

Farce: A type of comedy genre

Habitable: Good enough to live in

Indigenous: Native to a certain place

Metamorphosis: This word comes from the Ancient Greek word for 'transformation' and refers to the change in physical form that some animals undertake throughout their lives

Neuroscientist: Scientists who specialise in the brain

Nordic: A group of languages from the Nordic region in Northern Europe (Norway, Denmark, Finland, Sweden, Iceland & the Faroe Islands). Nordic can also refer to people from this region

Norsemen: Similar to Vikings, a group of people from Scandinavia during the Middle Ages

Oratory: The skill of public speaking

Superstitious: Believing in supernatural things (magic, ghosts, myths, witchcraft etc)

Paleontologist: Someone who studies fossils

Persian: The Persian Empire was previously one of the largest in the world. The country of Persia no longer exists (it is now Iran), but Persian can still refer to the ethnic group or the language (which is also known as Farsi)

Glossary

Pilgrimage: A journey of self-discovery

Poverty: A state of not having enough money for basic needs, such as food or housing

Psychiatrist: A doctor who specialises in mental health

Ostracised: Excluded/banished from society

Zoologist: Someone who studies animals and wildlife

Printed in Great Britain
by Amazon